PICKING UP
SIGNALS

With best wishes.
Jane

Jane Pearn

T

Troubador Publishing Ltd
Unit E2 Airfield Business Park,
Harrison Road, Market Harborough,
Leicestershire. LE16 7UL
Tel: 0116 2792299
Email: books@troubador.co.uk
Web: www.troubador.co.uk

ISBN 978 1836281 818

British Library Cataloguing in Publication Data.
A catalogue record for this book is available from the British Library.

Printed and bound in Great Britain by 4edge Limited
Typeset in 11pt Minion Pro by Troubador Publishing Ltd, Leicester, UK

For my families

Contents

My life as an untitled document

becomes too hard so I slip away.
My tongue is bleeding with questions.
what is my name   where do I belong

There are silver coins on the forest floor. I try
to lift them but their roots are deep.
I follow their trail to a pool of silence.
In it is a house, reflected. I flow through the door.
This house is empty, I think.
I fall asleep in a nest of twigs and slow-curling moss.

I wake to find myself surrounded. They read me,
these mothers, fathers, old ones, ancestors.
They ask where I am going, I tell them
nowhere that I know and they nod. I ask
is this where I belong   do you know my name
They smile and shake their heads.
The ancestors have kind voices and feed me broth.
They send me on my way, clutching the ticket they offer.
It is made of water. I lick it to cool my tongue.

Chosen

I *Congratulations*

Your order
is available for collection.
The sex is confirmed as female.
You should have a new name ready and
there will be some paperwork to complete.

Please note that returns
are not permitted.

Specifications of anything listed as
    > unwanted gift <
are based on report, which may not be
entirely accurate or honest.

Available information suggests:
    in working order
    average size
    dark hair
    grey eyes
    reasonably intelligent
    right-handed
    left-leaning

This does not constitute a guarantee. Furthermore
at any point during her lifetime she will be affected by
factors beyond her control, including but not limited to:

genetic errors
pre-delivery conditions
undisclosed history
usage
an abiding and intractable sense of loss

II *How it felt to be chosen*

Well now. To begin at the beginning. But where
does my beginning start? What about streets crossed, calls
missed, glances held, a stranger's smile returned?

Anyway.

I lost my parents. Or they lost me. More exactly
(it's important to be accurate: these matters
matter to me) they each, separately, left me.
He long before my birth and she at the moment
I breathed my first air. It was her intention
that I would not find my way home.
Newborns are not resourceful,
and there were no breadcrumbs.

Oh, I learnt the history.
Got herself pregnant (it's what they said)
couldn't feed an extra mouth.
Strangers owned my birth, wrote my story.
You were chosen balances (or not) the half of the equation
they didn't like to tell.
Say it, say it. *Not wanted.*

A transaction. A life delivered
with the sender's name redacted. A recipient, an address,
but it could have been anyone, anywhere. Chance.
They were over it sooner than I was. But then
they'd known for months. It was news to me.

In the photo my baby-face looks puzzled.
There's something wrong here. Different voice.
She doesn't smell right.
No mother-scented blanket to reassure.
No keepsake either, no pinned ribbon
to tell of her reluctance to part with me.
This isn't Dickens.

Pre-story: more than history. Who we were, before
we were. These were not my people. They wanted to,
but could not teach me belonging. Always the beloved guest,
I observed but couldn't know the thick complicity,
the stickiness of family; the ordinariness of looking-like.
How it would be to tell the pairs that came together
and together and together
to make the pair who made me.
I was a line-drawing, a 2-D sketch.
I had no bustle of ancestors, photos, faces, names,
names to faces. I was a character
lifted from a different book, a line from a different song.
Where there should be stories
there was silence.

Two lives. I wore her like borrowed clothes.
Sometimes I didn't answer to her name.

Or hesitated, a spy remembering my alias.

III *Interlude*

I grew up, grew away, raised children
who looked-like and took-after. Shall I
describe that quiet, private joy to you,
who take such things for granted?

IV *Found*

And then I found my mother.
You'll be hoping perhaps
for a happy ending.
The tears, the smiles, the relief.
The faces studied at arm's length,
the tale of regret, of understanding
sought and granted.
What they call closure.
You're going to feel cheated.

You were a mistake, that's all. No,
I won't name your father. It's none
of your business. Don't call again.

Yes, I felt the same.

Some silence is needed while we take this in.

Caught and thrown-back, I must live
with the barb embedded in my flesh.

5

V *Matryoshka*

And yet here we are, all of us.
A bewildered baby. A child escaping
into books. A lost and furious teenager.
My arms ache with the need to hold you.
I whisper a message down the years.
I'm looking at you and I am you.
You're safe inside me. I've got us.

There was always a distance

No, you would say, it's not true,
you weren't second-hand, second-best.
You were special.
You were chosen.

But you watched me
cradle my new-born's head,
still damp with my waters,
inhaling his scent which was my scent too,
and I heard your voice tremble
with fought-back tears.
I never had that, never will, you said.

And I knew I'd been right all along.

Blossom

I break bud, you flower. Here is the sweet blossom of you, palest mauve and silent, smeared with blood. They lay you on my breast, you who I've known for long months and not at all. Voices, *don't worry, he's fine.* I know it, I am not afraid. Through both our skins we feel your tiny pulse. You gasp, breathe air, pink outwards from the heart, blossom, colour unfurling to arms legs earlobes fingernails. You pause, consider before you utter (this will become a pattern) then give voice. You cry, I laugh, say welcome, hollowed out with love.

You go for a walk with your mother

We wind uphill, you with your long legs loping ahead. I pause often, catch my breath, apologise. You laugh at me, but kindly.

A peregrine's thin scream rips the sky, thrills our blood. There are quiet stars in the cropped grass: your shadow now out-lengthens mine, but I can still teach you the names of flowers.

A levelling path, a sudden corner turned. Loch Skeen, a piece of mirror dropped into the cleft of hills. We marvel at its ice-pure water, speculate about rocks and time.

You are restless, eager to explore; but I perch on a tussock sprung from dense dark peat, listen to the water's lap and ripple, watch the circles widen from a rock's jut.

Glancing up to find you vanished, I feel the sickening swerve behind the ribs that mothers of lost children know. I stand abruptly and see you across the water waving, already more distant than I had supposed.

Hoping

for parents of sick children

I carry my hope
in a leaky basket
woven from the willow
that grows against
the garden wall, the willow
I coppice each spring,
the tree that will not die.

I do not know how the story ends.
I do not know how we can bear this.
But I know that it is part of love
and inescapable.

My basket is heavy with hope.

Bridge passage

The walk not finished, I stop to lean
on this barely-a-bridge spanning only
a grassy track. To what purpose the span?

For what reason my pause?
Warm brick hums beneath my forearms,
breeze riffles the backs of my legs.

Ochre cliffs a field away fall to a silken sea.
The tide is in. I watch the gulls' screams
tear strips off cobalt sky,

leaving scrapes of white.
The bridge and I. In our shadows
tall grasses ache with seed,

vetch embroiders their stems with purple.
Plump honeyed clovers, guarded
by fierce nettles at the edge.

I stay although there is nothing much to see
because it is there, and I can,
and it may be the last time.

Even the grasses

I step into early morning, the road
        leading to (or from) somewhere
I need not be. Stonechats bob

and tease, daring me closer,
        always ahead, and anyway
have the advantage of wings. They should pity

the lumpen human tethered to earth by gravity
        and disappointment, lacking
the dimension of air, needing tracks.

A hare, startled, long-muzzled, elegant, converges
        sight-scent-sound
on the trespasser, lopes away.

A pair of yearlings roadside of the fence, frozen,
        each head a perfect Y of alarm and calculation.
Delicate hooves skitter on tarmac. In less

than a thought they gather muscle, tendon,
        bone, pour themselves upwards
over the wire; close to flying, too.

Go home, go home. I am a distracting pebble dropped
        into the quiet day. Something stirs the air
and even the grasses lean away.

Plague

At first they were afraid. They stayed behind their walls and they covered their faces. We took to their streets, loping, sniffing, exploring, tasting. Our roots split their concrete. They were still here, but not so many. And it was better: bats took the credit.

The few that remain alive are easily dealt with. But their leavings litter our space, stink the air, clog the seas. Now beetles and microbes get to work. The sky lightens, lifts, invents its own clouds. Blossoms erupt and six-eyed butterflies swim.

By little their paths close over, by little their buildings crumple, by little our tendrils reach. Trees grow where trees will. By little we reclaim. We do what we need and nothing more. Snakes go about their muscular business and apples are eaten for their flavour.

There is glisten and shine, shell and scale, feather and frill and fin, carapace and fur. Spotted, striped, reticulated. Tail and mane and tufted ears. Shoals and drifts, flocks and swarms and roaming packs. Hatching, dying, decaying, budding.

The nights are dark again and quiet. Quiet with the sound of insect feet, the whirr of wings, the fall of petals. Quiet with the pad of paws, and the rasp of teeth. Quiet with trickling water, the chafe of sand, a raindrop on a leaf.

Fresh rivers run to meet the sea and fish dance in coral reefs. Rocks boil and tilt and settle. Clean winds sculpt, water returns to ice. Moon-tides lap our shores, earth breathes.

Allium inter alia

Shortening days, and we are greyed out.
Nectar exhausted, abandoned by bees,
we fall silent into our own straw.

Now that we no longer please your eye
you cut us down. No matter,
we have done all that we intended.
We allowed the air to carry away our seeds,
but our hearts were always underground.

Our lives had their own importance.
Within us we carried our offspring and theirs,
and theirs. It was never only about us
here, now, in this garden,
but what comes next and next.

Street

On the gum-pebbled pavement outside Tesco
an old man is playing a didgeridoo.
It rests on his blanket, leans against his mouth
as if confiding a secret. Weathered and worn,
their skins both patterned with story.

His breathing circular as time
creates an endless deep warm deep brown hum
deep hum warm hum endless
hum on and on and on.

It is one note and many. Barnacled, mossed
with harmonies, it is the sound of thunder
and ocean and roots. It is like the earth calling
from beneath the tarmac.
It pulses through my feet, sings in the bone,
reminds me of something I can't quite know.

Ungainly, balanced on our strange two legs,
we walk the grey streets hunched, ear-phoned,
staring into screens.
Figures huddled in the doorway of the pub
take urgent, shallow puffs. Silent clouds
hover around their mouths.

Hanging baskets freighted with neon blooms
sway in the backwash of cars.
There are no trees. Under a shout of laughter
the earth hums its sad song.

A tough little wind muscles
through a gap, loiters aimlessly,
glances at broken bottles, crumpled flyers,
kicks a can. A plastic bag bellies, flutters
and falls. A child wails.

Shadows

In the garden, digging the warming earth.

Unquiet graves.

Robin perches close enough to touch, watches me
tear up roots, dispose unwanted lives.

Mariupol. Rafah.

Sparrows chatter, an intricate mesh
of sound, building this year's homes.

Gaping houses. Rubble. A shoe in the road.

Blackbird on chimney offers his song, oblivious.
Over the wall, children's voices in the playground.

Children's voices.

The sky is painted gold and blue and white.
Dandelions dazzle like small suns.

In the sky, an unseasonal mushroom.

Bright-eyed robin tilts inquiring head. *Well?*

I do not have an answer.

after Jill Bialosky

Because
April 1975, Phnom Penh

Because when the bombs fell on the people
their lives were lost and their homes were lost.

Because the red-scarfed ones with their tractor-tyre sandals
moved in and said help us; because

the red-scarfed ones said if you want to build
a new country, come to the hill. Because the doctors

& lawyers & engineers & teachers,
dancers & monks & poets who wanted to help

came to that hill and the red-scarfed ones
shot them all. Because it is Year Zero and there will be

no gods, no family, no money, no clocks,
no medicines from the west, no learning of any kind.

Because in the end a red-checked tablecloth
covered the green land, laid with two million skulls.

Red

*Tuol Sleng, 'Poison Hill'. Khmer Rouge interrogation centre,
once a school. Many of the guards were very young.*

Quiet. Heavy, still, remembering air.
Subdued footsteps on cracked floors.
Red tiles. No school now

but we have come to learn
at the place of the poison tree.
Petals drift, pink and white.

Hints of horror. Shackles, iron bed-frames.
Rusted pincers for the sudden
red flowering of fingernails.

A list of rules, translated for tourists.
When getting lashes or electrification
you must not cry at all.

Rough brick kennels in a classroom. Chains and bolts.
A stain, once red, on the wall.
Hearing the scented air bright with screams.

Do nothing, sit still and wait for my orders.
The harsh voices of dead-eyed barbaric children.

If there is no order, keep quiet.

Landmine

I've been here for years, forgotten after it was all over. For all I know, above me they're going about their lives in sunshine, with birdsong. There are others like me: in this silent crowd I am an actor waiting for my cue, my big moment.

They don't see me. How could they, buried as I am in soft soil? I don't see them either but if I sense vibration, I quiver a little: it's almost like excitement.

It's what I was made for. I'm calibrated to maim, not kill outright. So much more impact. The screams, ripped flesh, splintered bones, the rescuers' fear – my designers were thoughtful, they imagined this.

Unless it's a child: too small, too soft for the desired effect. About these matters I have no opinion, I make no choices. A footfall is all I need.

I wait. I am patient, never tired, will not die. Unless. Then I die with them: this I know. Perhaps it will be a little one who chases a butterfly, runs towards me. Or a father who finds me when he digs. What are the odds? For both of us, the chance of a lifetime.

In perpetuum

Tulips open as
red wounds: bomb-deaths each contain
seeds of war to come.

War opens wounds: each
death contains bombs to come, as
seeds of red tulips.

Each bomb-death to come
contains seeds of war: tulips
open, red as wounds.

English lesson, verbs

We lived in Syria. People were fighting
and we could not stay. We came
to Scotland. We left
our son behind. We cried.

The strange syllables clang like bells,
itemise our sorrows, iterate them.

The past is not finished, it lives
in every awakening in this house
of unfamiliar brick we try to call home,
in this land of smiles and rain, where
the sun does not keep its promises.
Our sun was never like this.

We try to stay in the present. We go
to English classes, we walk
to the shops. In our dreams we taste
falafel and dates. We hope
to return to the time before. We know
that we can't.

We do not have the tenses we need.

This should never have happened.
It might have been different.
What will become of us?

Yes, but the children

Round and round the garden
goes the teddy bear,
but this little piggy went to market.
The next didn't and that proved wise
in the circumstances.
The third did all right for himself,
the fourth went hungry.
And the littlest one, inevitably,
cried wee-wee-wee all the way home.

Another little piggy went to market his idea
for making money out of houses.

Here's hoping, said the mother as she rolled the dice
and bought a mansion for Park Lane
where no one could afford to stay.
Invisible people were evicted from the houses
even in the cheaper streets.
They were tipped back into the box
with the sellotaped corners and forgotten
until next Christmas.

There was no garden now to go round,
so the children played hopscotch,
and soldiers, and tag, up and down the street.
The lamppost on the corner was called Home.
Sunlight played too on the chalked pavement,
then down came the rain and washed poor Incy out.
Not that anybody noticed.

And the winter nights were thin sheets
and black damp, and no money for the meter.
And the summer days were outgrown
clothes, and only bread for tea,
and city dirt between the baby's toes.
Which brings us back to the little piggy
and all that he led to.

After the revolution

After the revolution, guns will be laughable
and we will not be afraid to be kind.

We will acknowledge the stars with our heads bowed,
and thank the moon for tides.

After the revolution, flowers will have an opinion.
They will express this forcefully as they surge

from their buds into the light. After the revolution,
I shall listen to whispering forests

and in a small notebook covered with lemonskin
I shall write down the stories trees tell about us.

I shall read these aloud to anyone
who will listen and even – especially – if they won't.

Unending

At that moment I died and my body swung away from me
like a heavy sack. Of course I resisted, a child
fighting sleep, a leaf fearing the fall.
But when I had to let go, my relief was great.
How burdened I had been, believing that it was I, I it.

All that had been clear, the lichened oak tree,
birdsong, the walls of my house, melted into mist.
The people in my story – their faces, what I had felt for them –
darkened and drifted away.

At first I didn't understand and I missed time.
I had believed it was real, an after to before,
a signpost to a destination. Now I know

that when I thought my life begun and ended,
it had always been what it must forever
be a part of – a world spinning for no reason
but itself, and I a transient arrangement of atoms,
returned to the dark oblivion of soil, the salty ocean,
my voice a note in the song the wind sings.

Stand at the edge

The shore. The land's frayed hem. Where
certainty is worn down grain by grain,
where knowing (you thought you did) meets
unknowable (now you know that you don't).
Stand at the edge of the seeming-solid world (but
sands roll rub shift beneath bare soles)
watch the perpetual restlessness of sea
feel its pulses echo at the wrist.
It has its own life, its own reasons,
(your life came from it, your atoms will return)
it has no need of you.
Take a paint-box. Could you? Do it? Glass-deep
green, blue of long summers-ago, silver of promises
nearly-kept. Pigments to capture colours
that are not colours at all like (tones moods airs)
adventure, longing, pity, home.
How to depict the crump – hear it, feel it –
as waves fold over themselves
too heavy for their own strength,
drive against cliff?
Find the wordpaint (can you?) for
how it would be to smooth your palm over
the swelling liquid pillow,
to stroke its curve's expand and stretch.
For how it arches – a horse's neck – along its length,
shatters. A billion bubbles. For how
each captures the sky, explodes
with light, dies exhausted. For how
the foam's shed skin returns to sea. Begins again.

after Mary Oliver

Another little owl poem

Late. Dark. The road's an oiled black stream
between tall hedges. I am humming that poem.

Ahead on the tarmac, plumb on the dotted line,
something upright, dappled. My heart stops

before my wheels. What if I hadn't seen you?
If I had rubbed you to a scribble

of bone and flesh, written your end in bloodied quills?
I could not have borne the shame of it.

I ease the door, my cautious footfalls stroke the road.
High now in the hawthorn, you are expecting me.

Ink-pool eyes in neatly feathered face unblinking
watch me. Perhaps you were flagging me down.

I look, you look. We lock. I wait.
Ten seconds and all my life. What message?

Enough. You nod once, spread those soft bright sails,
float skyward. I would have stayed and stayed.

sparrow

arrives in a blink
  lands light as a coat of dust
    bounces on spindle legs
sharp glance around
     dips head
neat stab at crumb of moving soil
  tilts neck
    bright berry eye
lace-strutted shoulders lift wings
      airborne
flurry into hawthorn
  blends with dapple and chorus

old doctor

shrugs grey gown around
hides ragged edges looks respectable
waits for plump sleek silvers
no appointment but they'll come
they'll come

watches   still   like stone

there

stab
sharp through waterskin
fastidious forceps lift sleek silver (plump)
brisk necktwistflick arranges longwise
silver down red gape headfirst slithers
not time enough to airdrown
tail protesting side to side

unhitches his gown
flaps untidy sleeves
rises belly-full

scatter of scales burnishes water

but i am crow

i don't sing
    or chirp or
  warble

who needs music?

i scrape
        i scrape like the gravel
in my gizzard   like there's sand
        in my heart
with my voice i scour the air
i rasp the blue
            off the sky

who needs pretty?
                who needs charm?

see my strong black quills
    tough beak
            my noticing eye
my tilt and listening head

            i smell the blood
                i judge the speed of cars

i get what i want
            the flesh   the bones

    i leave when i am ready

my deliberate wings

Madame Trotsky sashays down the stairs

or pours herself like upward water to
a tiny ledge   pauses   poised

the plume of her tail poses questions   or maybe
scarfs her ankles   or   hangs
like a bookmark in time

her fur is longer than her lick   and
its scent is warm biscuit

she tastes my tears   softly bites
my fingers   spoons me in sleep

shares my yoga mat
and does not   I think   laugh
at my ungrace

she carries her own points
keeps them sharp   uses
to brake   or   seize

but mostly her hours are
unpunctuate
            and silver
                  flow

Tweed

This wandering trickle of mercury
   on the map, this liquid road,
path and traveller both,

   patient (has no lifetime), shapes
hills, gouges valleys, seeks to redefine
   its borders – recognises none of ours.

Left to itself unbounded would have
   no edge – spread molecule-thin,
would gauze the land with water.

Confined, asks relentless questions
  of its banks, tests
   for weakness,
  combs through grasses,
 eases soil
from roots, invisibly shifts
  mud-sludge, gravel-grains.

Defies the odds
  against it,
argues with rock
  and wins.
   Eventually.

In spate, rips at the
    restraint of channels, in
        impartial rage lifts trees,
          enters houses,
    exacts payment
for its long imprisonment.

Yearns toward the sea,
    tumbles in eagerness
   to bring perpetual gifts, silt and stone,
souvenirs of the journey it can't help making.

Sea honours the tribute, shifts and sighs,
exhales her gratitude in clouds, feeds the giver.

pebble under lens

cracked and cratered   pocked like acned skin
   it darkens with a lick of spit
dries and fades again to rose

a cool egg of sand compressed by aeons
   resting   after all this time
on the warm map of my palm

Mood board

A wooden table, sullen
with knife-scars. In a chipped vase,
a swagger of tulips.

A crumpled note *what's done
can't be undone.* A slow breath,
a crimson petal, fallen.

Keeper

Excuse me I said
as I tripped on the tongue
rubbery and pink-flecked
on the hall carpet.
I thought at first
it must be licking up crumbs but no, it was
talking – something about leaving
but it didn't make sense
so I nudged it, hard,
with my steel-capped toe.

It was nearly at the door before me.
Careful I said *you don't want
to get trapped.* I stepped over
its quivering tip
into the sunshine,
locked it in
and left it still talking,
asking, imploring.

?

You would confront it but
it slinks around the corner
of the library smearing the windows with
words that leach from the bricks,
trail behind it like thick chattering smoke.

It stands below you in the shadow
of bridges (you cross each one as you come
to it). The waters are troubled.

It taps you on the shoulder.
Hot and urgent breath. Cunning,
you don't turn round but reach a hand back
to grab its coat which falls in flat
felted folds from your fingers
while it laughs hunched into a question
in the next street.

Still

The shrill alarm has razored sleep,
torn the fabric of my dreams.

I lie still, consider the slanting skylight,
its edges a frame for itinerant clouds.

Letting the world manage, as it does, without me.

The sky's light is in the room. It falls
on the drawer not shut, on the waiting clothes,

on the mirror framing the frame. The glass
contains the same unhurried clouds.

Sparrows squabble. Uneven footfalls - high heels in a hurry.
A lorry reverses. Voices are loud then fade.

Thinking how busy it all is, how we go on with the necessary things.

A dog barks twice. Somewhere
beyond the edge of the page, a door closes.

Geometry lesson, long ago

in
that
hot glass
box of summer
classroom, drowsy
with the drone and scent
of cut grass – seeing with new
eyes the right angle of each corner,
a diagonal shaft of dusty light – I intone
the theorem, entranced by the word hypotenuse

Moon blood

You were twelve. You found
a rust-red teardrop in your knickers.
You were surprised, but not. Your mother said
it was called the Curse. She didn't say why.

You felt scared that you were a woman.

You dreaded the dull blade-scrape drag,
the seep of blood to your face too
as you asked to be excused.
But you had joined the sisterhood.

You felt proud that you were a woman.

Your body had been an unconsidered thing
that ran and played and climbed.
Now it needed tending.

You felt betrayed.

Feeding swans

My grandpa would take me to feed the swans.
One hand clutched my paper bag of crusts,
the other his. Skipping to keep up
while avoiding the cracks.

Down the concrete ramp
to a river more effluent than stream,
its water seeping from the factories, a skin of scum,
brown bubbles caught in eddies.

I loved the swans and feared them,
their powerful wings, their snake-like necks.
Mistaking the nostrils in their orange beaks for eyes,
to me they seemed angry, forced to live

in this filth, their whiteness a reproach.
I threw my bread as far as short arms could, wanting
to appease, afraid they might rise from the water
to snatch it (once, one had stepped on to the bank –

it stood as tall as me). The crumbs shaken out,
we turned away. Until we reached the corner, I'd look
over my shoulder, just in case, fearing
some kind of retribution.

Concert piece

On concert nights she becomes a stranger.
We are not her children but tasks
to be completed. Answers are perfunctory,
meals hasty. She is withdrawing

to a distant land. We have no passport.
I play on the floor outside
the music room. She sketches out a phrase, scribbles
tiny variations on the air, repeats, repeats.

Tight-tucked sheets keep me face-up for the bedtime kiss.
Fur brushes my cheek, a vapour trail
– camphor and violets – follows the closing door.
I inhabit orphaned dreams, jealous of a piano's toothy smile.

At a stroke

Bewildered. But speech remains.
You have to get me out of here, I have a concert.
Oh if I could, but the blown pupil says no.
A deep wide pool of nothing, thin-ringed by iris.

Habit's solid towers – how to use a leg,
a hand – have crumpled, intricate synapses uncoupled,
connections lost.

I imagine (try not to) a bloody tide
breaching the defences, swirling past
the sole inhabitant. Detritus in the flood.

   holiday snaps   a piano

key   the way home   a melody   those red

     shoes   a page of Keats

  daffodils   C minor

The beautiful mechanism lies vandalised,
beyond repair. Yesterday
your fingers danced for Mozart.

***

You are dreaming awake and restless.
My words   I can tell   start to make no sense
slip off their skins of meaning   leave bare
bones of   stops and   vowels and
sibilants. You seem puzzled, search my face.

Nurses change the drip. I switch to music.
Pour Beethoven's Spring Sonata   the joy of it   into
your ear. Speech remains. A crooked smile,
a hand on mine, pressing.

***

Two days and two nights.
Your longest diminuendo, beautifully judged.
Into silence.

I am holding my breath, like you. I am waiting for you
to lift your hands from the keyboard,
the pause, the applause.

Nearly

I should have been angry with you,
I should have shouted. Strangers linked
by a chance of timing, you and I had been
one violent reflexive swerve away
from a very different day.

I'm sorry you said *I didn't see you.*
I'm so sorry. Your chin quivering
with the suddenness and fright of it.

We stood unshelled beside the cars.
Seeing the softness of our bodies, the frailty
of bone, the sudden beauty of untorn skin,

It's OK, I said, *We're both OK.*
Nothing happened.

Fallen

You remember falling,
but not how instinct made you
turn away your head, angle an elbow
to take the brunt.

You tried to save yourself,
and failed. Tomorrow
bruises will blossom
in places you thought untouched.

Afterwards

Mostly you keep it at bay
with the blade you didn't know
you grip between white tight knuckles.
And it helps that sullen brain refuses
to meet your eye, resists remembering.

So you're fine, you're OK, until
a word, an image, a certain scent,
a something you couldn't foresee, and
you're there again. All the days,
months, years, since it happened
have folded into each other

and then is sudden now.
For all the running you need to do
your limbs are weighted with rage and fear.
You can't leave, you can't bear to stay.

Now the precarious egg has fallen,
and all the king's horses and certainly not his men.
Your distress lies exposed on the carpet
for everyone to see and you can't
gather it up all raw and slippery,
the way it is with hot tears and snot,
can't put it back in its neat-and-tidy shell.

You stand empty staring at the mess
– embarrassment all round –
it's broken, you are, and can't be
and you can't see how it can be
mended, ever.

For Joey

He is a bruised peach, that indentation
in the centre of his forehead

the record of his last encounter
with the solidity of objects.

Staggering from chair to table
in newfound uprightness

he learns the hard (the only) way
about the world and its edges

and how although he knows himself invincible
he will always be softer than circumstance,
marked by chance encounter.

Walking up to high school

There's one doesn't quite manage it.
He scuffs and scowls with the others,
cultivators of the stony stare,
guardians of the distance between our worlds.
But greeted by a stranger a little like his mum,
forgets himself. *Hello* he says and smiles.
Then, remembering his manners,
he frowns at the pavement, blushing.

Coming home

The students are coming home for Christmas.
Some have green hair and are fatter
because of chips and pot noodles.
Some are thinner because of love.

They wonder at the smallness of the buildings
and smile at the displays in the little shops.
Their bodies don't fit the bed like before
and the wall posters are embarrassing.

For a day or two they can't find the teabags.
Their mother has forgotten how much they eat
and has to send out for supplies.
One has gone vegan and didn't think to say.

Their thumbs are busy talking even while
they answer the neighbours' questions.
There is an argument.
They wonder at the smallness of their parents.

Remembering Riccarton

Memories uncouple with the passing years.
You summon the ghosts of men
you knew. Some of them return.
Big Jimmy the Shunter, Duncan the Goodsman.

Riccarton Junction. High and hidden
from the world, a landlocked island
of railway trades, caught in a tracery of tracks.

Still in your sleep you'll hear the rhythmic tick
of distant wheel on rail, the clang and clatter
of the yards, the great beasts coming in
like huge dogs panting, the thin scream of steam released.

Always the tang of metal in your mouth like blood, the acrid stink
of coal, the neighbours as close as a wet Monday's washing.
Your pride – just thirteen and one of the men.

But you forget the times you'd longed for a wider world.
The dreaming moments when you lifted your eyes
to those desolate moors, when you understood
that the rails outlast the journey, that past your station
they might have taken you anywhere.

At Moniack Mhor

Such rain. We're marooned in mist, beclouded,
horizoned by ridges we won't climb. At least

not today, when green merges with grey and
cloud-rims might be mountains.

Droplets cascade from an inconsolable
sky, runnel off roofs and ledges in

dripping syncopated rhythm.
On the gravelled path, water finds a way,

forces tiny stones aside to form
a provisional riverbed, widens

like some miniature Voltava, seeking
(as it always does) its level, hunting for the sea.

Water chafes at the land as words rub at
what we really mean, dislodge particles

of thought and draw them towards
the open mouth, the waiting pen.

woke up this morning

words everywhere
              in my hair
        in the creases of the sheets
    slid into curling piles on the floor
              under my nails
    between my legs

they'd been dreaming they could dance

    could sing   might capture
        the fizz and spangle of half-formed thoughts
    become chords and
              layers
          and harmonies

and now
          but now
they trudge across the page in sullen single file

The reading

The writer asserts her moral right
to be considered the author of these words,
or at least their order since none of them
are new-hatched, and to read them aloud
as she pleases.

Furthermore, she declares her right
to share a meal with other poets,
(some stranger than fiction) and be
unacquainted with the nudging thigh,
the sweaty hand below the table
fumbling towards her lap.

And while she's about it,
and although she should not need to,
she insists on the right to amble back alone
to the affordable guest house, juggling words
in her head or just wondering,
through well-lit streets or even darkened alleys,
oblivious of footsteps. And not
be seen as an opportunity,
or a target, or even *god help us* prey.

At a window

I could have been out last night,
stargazing. It was clear enough,
the air still, frost forming constellations
on the dark path. But I curtained off
the sky and turned my back. In truth,
I was afraid of infinity.

This morning I am joining the dots
of the sheep that stud the hill
that leans against the town,
searching for a shape
like a plough or a bear.
Or a word perhaps, a message.

Autumn aubade

Morning has fractured my warm and pillowed dreams.
You were there. I tap the alarm into silence
but light grazes my eyelids. The cat shifts
on my legs and sings a small song.

Down the winding stair with winding cat
into the sleeping kitchen. I haul up the blind,
surprise the sun peering through the glass.
Embarrassed, it retreats behind a cloud.

The water in the kettle dances, toast
scents the air, the radio murmurs news and music.
I cradle my cooling mug of tea,
search for a face in the table's familiar knots.

The day is rousing itself. Trees are bending
and stretching, loosened leaves are dizzy
with wind. Fallen apples stud the grass
like rubies. You should be here.

what is missing

is touch — is cotton to wool, sheer
to slub
        is holding hands

is hug — forms moulding each
to each, body to body
        rise to hollow

what is missing is skin warm against
cool, is the cheek-scuff
        of familiar stubble

is rough sunbrown finger tracing
delicate never-seen-daylight crease
        what is missing is

the warm air of whisper in her ear — is folding
into the scent of him — is the long weight
        of his arm

across her shoulders like a bracket ending
this

Over

The waiter brings us coffee.
The sun is shining. I stare
through panoramic windows
at the mountains. In dark crevices
are cold white grudges
the sun won't reach.

I think of rats and how we are never
more than ten words away from an argument.
You look towards me over the rim
of the thick china cup.
Steam mists your glasses, and I can't
picture the exact colour of your eyes.
You place the cup back on the saucer,
make tiny adjustments as if the handle
must face due north.
You glance at your phone and tell me
the signal keeps dropping. I say I know.

Gone

The tap is not dripping.
    I check the windows and leave.
The doors are all locked.

I sit on the bus and wait for a thought.
    Nothing comes.
The tap is not dripping.

I look out at the muddy fields
    and write a note to myself.
The doors are all locked.

I take out your photo, the faded one,
and try to remember your voice.
    The tap is not dripping.
    The doors are all locked.

Grit

I took it off to shake,
expected the plink and roll
of tiny stone on tiles.

But nothing.

Snugged shoe back on foot,
took another step.

Still there.

Again, I looked and shook
more thoroughly, my sole knowing
what eyes did not.

Is it just me?

An image from a fairy-tale,
the pea impossibly cushioned
but still felt. The princess proving
her refinement – or unfitness for the world.

Get used to it.

It nags at each step, a small insistent pain.
I don't forget you.

Premonitory

This will be so: I will die on a Tuesday
   in winter as the light fades.
The roads will be gleaming.

It will happen quite suddenly
   on a road that gleams
with a slick of evening rain.

It will not be the fault of the cyclist
   slicked with evening rain,
or the lorry driver who will nudge me.

But I will slide across the carriageway
   although he only nudges me
into a blaze of glass

and wet fractured lights.
   After the blaze of glass has swallowed me
I will hear the wail of sirens.

I will lie cold, listening
   to the wailing sirens
which will not be unexpected.

Roads will gleam wetly, light will be fading
   – I am expecting this –
and I will die on a Tuesday, in winter.

Self-portrait, late period

Here, I am watching myself in the mirror,
the familiar stranger I've harboured all my life
who looks like someone I should know
but can't quite place. I lift my (so does she)
tee shirt and start to sketch. A skinscape,
crease and curve, a gardener's tan. The rest
is indoor-pale, surprised by light. I describe
with soft pencil the scars where she has bled
into the world, note a fold of breast, a belly
still marked with tracks of silver.
A pulse ticks in her neck. Then. Done.
Past. Gone. Regrets in the gaps, like shadows.
I try to see behind the eyes that watch me
looking. Here, I am.

Older

My hair used to grow sensibly. Understanding
that a parting was only temporary,

it would lie on either side of it without an argument.
Now it is growing grey, and wilful. It knows

no rules, changes its mind from one day
to the next, will not tolerate separation.

Multi-directional, it picks up signals from everywhere.

Marriage lines

He tells a joke and forgets the punchline.
He still thinks it's funny.

His knees hurt
but not as much as my ears.

He boils an egg with an inappropriate flourish.
He drops it.

He says he can't help snoring.
I say I can't help minding.

I offer him my hand to hold.
He turns away because *People might see us.*

He has a cold,
so he is limping.

When he's worried, he laughs.
When he laughs, I'm worried.

I am not the person he thinks I am.
Nor is he.

He says it hurts to breathe.
I tell him *Stop it, then.*

In a layby,

cans, a broken bottle, pizza vouchers,
flyers for past events. A baby's rattle, a single shoe.
A pheasant's iridescent feather, its crushed body.
The dark plantation behind, the hard grey road.
Cow parsley brushes our fingers, which are almost
fists. The pea jacket you wouldn't wear hangs,
all buttoned-up, from a gorse bush; in the pocket,
a packet of lozenges, the kind that actors use
before they perform. We stare at the ground.
One of us is missing and I don't know who.

In which I go too far

I have set my heart on the sea. It is a long way off but I reckon
I know how to find it. I travel best without a map.

Mazy lanes are edged with keep-out walls. All doors are closed,
eyeless windows stare at me. I am not afraid.

There. I knew it. A smudged pencil line between the trees.
I go on, and on, until water nudges my toes.

I remove my heart. This is not as difficult as you might think,
or as painful. Once it is free of its attachments it is

surprisingly light. It is smaller than I had supposed
and not as heart-shaped, unbroken but pale like cloud.

The tide is leaving the beach and all the little wavelets
are rosy-tipped with sun. I set my heart gently on the water and

let it go. I know the rules of the sea. *Rescued persons*
to be treated humanely and delivered to a place of safety.
I believe this also applies to hearts.

Acknowledgements

I am grateful to the editors of several magazines for publishing some of these poems: Ink, Sweat & Tears, Brittle Star, Spelt, Snakeskin, Dreichmag, ArtemisPoetry, The Lake, The Eildon Tree, Quantum Leap, Paperboats, and the Three Brethren newsletter. Other poems were included in the anthologies Border Voices and Sounding Voices. Earlier versions of four poems were included in my second collection, Further To.

Still was one of the winners in the 2018 Guernsey International Poems on the Move competition. *At a Stroke* was longlisted in the 2018 National Poetry competition, and placed second in the 2019 Against the Grain competition. An earlier version of *Plague* was longlisted in the 2020 National Poetry Competition, and in the 2021 Rialto Nature and Place Competition. It was Highly Commended in the 2024 McLellan Poetry Competition.

My thanks go to Carolyn Dowley, Richard Myers, Annie Maclean, Alison Cohen, Leonie Charlton, Susan Elsley and Frances Ainsley for their poetic company over the past four years. To Sophia Blackwell for her wise counsel. To Tom Murray, Anne Ryland, Caroline Bird and many others, for their encouragement and advice, and to the members of Borders Stanza for their constructive comments.

Biographical note

Jane Pearn was born in 1953 in London. In her twenties, she moved to the Isle of Man, where she home-educated her four children, helped run a plant nursery, set up a charity to support landmine clearance in Cambodia, and worked as a paediatric Speech and Language Therapist. In 2006 she moved to Selkirk in the Scottish Borders, where she still lives, with a cat called Florence.

Previous publications include *A Change of Error* (Autolycus Press); *Matters Arising* and *Further To* (Siskin Press); *The Language of Leadings* (Quaker Books).